THE GLORY OF LIGHT

PHOTOGRAPHS BY
ROBERT COOPER

AN ILLUSTRATED COLLECTION OF NEW PRAYERS

DAVID ADAM

Published in Great Britain in 2003 by
Society for Promoting Christian Knowledge
Holy Trinity Church
Marylebone Road
London NW1 4DU

Photographs © Robert Cooper 2003
Text © David Adam 2003

British Library Cataloguing-in-Publication Data
A catalogue record for this book is available
from the British Library

ISBN 0-281-05611-0

1 3 5 7 9 10 8 6 4 2

Designed and typeset by Theresa Maynard
Printed in China by New Era Printing Company Ltd

FOREWORD

For thirteen years I had the privilege of opening St Mary's church on Holy Island early in the morning. Often the interior was ablaze with a bright white light. There were times when it was as if something special was happening, and so it was for those with eyes to see. There were days when the whole island was vibrant with a light that was almost too bright for the eye, again giving the feeling that something else was about to emerge or happen. At such moments, I often remembered that the early church at Whithorn was known as 'Candida Casa' which means the 'White House' or 'House of Brightness'. On the opposite coast was Whitby, which means much the same; its even earlier name meant 'lighthouse'. I then rejoiced that I belonged to such a place of brightness and often recited or sang the hymn 'Immortal, invisible' with emphasis on the words

''Tis only the splendour of light hideth thee.'

Each day I try to capture the newness and freshness of the day, to wonder at what is all about me and to accept the otherness of creation. I enjoy the changing of light at each moment, on hills, sea or trees and know that I will never see them quite the same again. I am aware of the mystery and wonder of all that is about me and I know that anyone who takes the time can rejoice in and enjoy the miracle of creation. Take the time, for a person without wonder is a person not truly alive. Be aware of the glory of light that is around you until you know it is also within you.

Robert Cooper uses his camera as an artist to see into the beyond, and to help us to stop and wonder. Robert can come to a shallow pool in the sand and see great depths. His camera helps us to see not only with the eyes but also with the heart. His skill is to help us to regard the world around us with new vision and to bow before its mystery and its beauty.

Take your time. Look at the world about you. Wonder and enjoy the glory of light.

DAVID ADAM

BEGINNINGS

Lord, the day is cold
Warm it with your presence
The way is dark
Lighten it with your grace

Our hearts are empty
Fill them with your love
Our minds are fearful
Strengthen them with your hope

Our lives are sinful
Guide us in your way
Lord, we are yours
Be with us evermore

THE BEAUTY OF GOD

If we walk through the world
And do not see its beauty
If we cannot stop for a flower
How can we know you, Lord?

You speak to us through beauty
Let us reverence the spotted burnet
And look in awe upon the bugloss
Bowing before you in wonder

Lord, speak to us through light
Let us glimpse your splendour
May we thrill at your brightness
And be aware of your glory

Let all of your creation speak
And tell us of your power
Let us walk in gentleness
Among the mysteries you have made

THE GLORY OF LIGHT

Lord of glory
How can I remain dull
When bathed in your brightness?
Why am I not radiant
With your love and light about me?

Lord of love, fill my life
Dispel my darkness
Lighten my way
As the new dawn breaks
Let your sun rise in my heart

True light of the world
Enter the depths of my life
Flood the dark and hidden places
Overflow my whole being
With the light of your glory

THE PEACE OF THE PRESENCE

I asked for peace
you offered your presence

I asked for hope
you came to my side

I asked for joy
you lit my journey

I asked for love
you gave me yourself

GOD OF LIGHT

Light of lights
Come into the dark places of our hearts
Come and scatter the darkness
God of promise and hope
As we delight in the rainbow
May we ever trust ourselves to you
As the rainbow reaches to the heavens
Let us know we are one with you
We are under your protection
We live in the splendour of your light
You offer us your glory and yourself
Come, Lord, lighten our darkness
Renew our faith and our hope
For truly our hope is only in you

LORD OF GLORY

Lord of glory and holiness
I bow in wonder before you
I cannot capture the sunrise
How can I contain you?
I am unable to grasp the wind
How can I hold on to you?
Nowhere near touching the stars
How can I reach out to you?
God of deep mystery
Beyond our imagining
You reach out to us
You touch our lives
Still my mind and heart
That I may reflect your glory

DAILY DEDICATION

Let this day be
Full of your beauty and brightness
Lord, hear us

That we may know
Your presence and your peace
Lord, hear us

That we may experience
Your grace and your glory
Lord, hear us

That we may be at one
With you and your creation
Lord, hear us

That we may be aware of you
In and through and above all things
Lord, hear us

RESURRECTION DAY

The brightness of the dawning
Tells of Christ this morning
The sun sings of his birth
For Christ has come to earth
Each flower newly sprung
Speaks of his resurrection
Lord, give us grace to see
Your glory and divinity
And awaken us this day
To meet you on the way

HIDDEN DEPTHS

Lord, we have hidden depths
Unseen and unknown qualities
Our secret security and strength
Are rooted in the firmness of faith

Open the eyes of our hearts
To see beyond what is visible
May we sense more than we touch
And grasp more than we comprehend

Let our whole lives vibrate with your power
Our whole being respond to your presence
For we are always immersed in you
We are surrounded by your deep love

CORDS
OF LOVE

In the stillness
I look for you
I long for you
In my idleness
I watch for you
I wait for you
Our lives are interwoven
Use me as you will
We are bound together
In you I am strong
Every strand of my life
Is filled with your presence
In your hands, my life
Has purpose and meaning
Bind me close, Lord
With cords of love

GOD MY ROCK

O mighty and eternal God
You are as mysterious as the sea
I cannot understand you
If I remain on the shore
I cannot grasp your depth
Whilst standing in the shallows
You say, 'Thrust out from the land.
Launch out into the deep.'
I put my hand in yours, Lord
Now let me enter the darkness
Now let me walk in the deep
Let your mystery enfold me
And your presence uphold me
Among the rocks and waves
And through every storm

REFLECTED GLORY

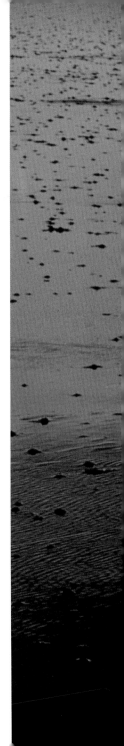

As the wet sands
Can hold the clouds
And reflect the sun
So may my life
Reveal your beauty
And reflect your glory

As the darkened earth
Takes on the light
And is full of a new radiance
So may the darkness of my life
Absorb your love
And radiate your presence

GOD MY FORTRESS

God my stronghold and might
Grant me your protection
And help me rise above all
That would bring me down

Give me of your strength
And in strength confidence
And in confidence knowledge
And in knowledge love of you

Then in my love for you, Lord
A deep love for your creation
God my stronghold and might
Grant me your protection

TRANSFIGURATION

We come disfigured
Disturbed, disgusted
We come with little hope
With fear and anxiety
To you, Risen Lord
Quickener of the dead

In you we are renewed
In you we have peace
In you we are loved
In you we have hope
You, Lord, are our life
You are our salvation

THE PASSING STORM

Lord God
You are as mighty as the ocean
As mysterious as the sea
In the storm I called upon you
But I did not see you
I cried out above the waves
But no relief, no help came
I sought for comfort in distress
My faith wavered at each blast
The rocks felt close and dangerous
I asked for healing of my pain
Are you there, Lord?
Are you aware, Lord?
Come walk the waves
Still my storm

THE WAY OF GOD

When I walk in the shadows
Unsure of my way
When I fail to see the beauty
Or the wonders about me
Come, Lord, guide me into light
Show me the way to walk in

Lord, go before me and lead me
Let me follow in your steps
Then let me boldly venture
Rejoicing in all about me
Reveal to me the way of holiness
And the glories of your creation

NEVER CAST
AWAY

Spirit of God
Brooding over the waters
Renew and re-use us

Wind of God
Sweeping over the world
Restore and revive us

Breath of God
Filling all things
Refresh and inspire us

Power of God
Bringing order out of chaos
Work in and through us

THE LIGHT
OF LIFE

We wait in the dawn
Until your light is within us
Lord, let your deep joy
Shine out from our eyes
Grant that your wisdom
Will inspire us with brightness
Let the splendour of your glory
Glow out through our actions
Come and burn within us
Until we radiate your light
Capture our cold hearts
Set us ablaze with your love
Change us and we shall be changed
Lord, fill us with the light of life

THE EYES OF THE HEART

Lord, help me this day
To look into the depths
And see with the heart
To behold the miracle of life
To rejoice in the mystery of growth
To bow before the otherness of creation
To love the uniqueness of everything
To accept the strangeness of all
Give me, Lord, the joy of seeing
Of looking with the eyes of the heart

ALONE ON A HILL

Christ
Guide to the lost
Peace to the storm-tossed
Light in our darkness
Safe haven for travellers
Let us not be useless
Or lacking purpose

Healer of the sick
Hope of the hopeless
Lover of the rejected
Restorer of life
Let us not rust away
Revive us and use us

Come, Lord of life
Reveal in us your glory

THE ABIDING PRESENCE

How strange it is
I search for you
When you are with me
I seek your presence
Whilst dwelling in you
I look for your love
When I am in your heart
I ask for protection
Whilst you walk with me
I ask for peace
When it lies unused within me

Let me know I abide in you
And you are ever in me

AFTERWORD

One morning in church we were listening to St Paul's words, 'God, who is rich in mercy, out of the great love with which he loved us, even when we were dead through our trespasses, made us alive together with Christ.' At that very moment the early morning sunlight burst through the clear glass of the east window. Sitting towards the back, I was treated to a vision of heads aflame with light. A moment before everyone had seemed quite unremarkable. Yet now the halo they wore showed their true value and standing in the sight of God. Perhaps most humbling of all was to think that, for someone sitting behind me, my head too would be crowned with light.

It has taken me many years of thinking of myself as a 'miserable sinner' to realize that my primary vision of myself should be as God sees me: 'in Christ'. So I was struck when I encountered Thomas Merton's conviction that 'no human being is "Life's poor creation". We are loved by Love precisely for being the fallible, fragile creatures that we are.'[1] Note that. Not 'in spite of' our fallible fragility, but 'because' of it.

That vision is reinforced for me by a number of the photographs in this book. Take, for example, the shed window. What attracted my eye was what was 'wrong' with it – the peeling paint that the tidy householder in me might have wanted to burn off and replace. I loved its texture, which was so much more interesting than if it had been pristine. The other thing that makes the picture is the broken pane. The damage breaks the rhythm and offers a point of focus. I now realize that I loved what I saw not in spite of, but precisely because of the imperfection and damage.

Light is what reveals such imperfections, but the light of God is never merciless as J. R. Peacey's hymn reminds us:

'Before his cross for guidance kneel;
his light will judge and, judging, heal.'

As St Paul sees it, that healing judgement is performed as we gaze into the glorious light of Christ's face and, incredibly, generously, find our fallible, fragile spirits transformed 'from one degree of glory to another'.[2]

ROBERT COOPER

1. *The Intimate Merton* edited by Patrick Hart and Jonathan Montaldo, Lion, 1999, p. 16
2. 2 Corinthians 3.18